Love is Never Wasted

Love is Never Wasted

Carol D. Patterson

Copyright © 2008 by Carol D. Patterson.

ISBN: Softcover   978-1-4363-3259-0

All rights reserved. No part of this book may be reproduced or transmitted in any form or by any means, electronic or mechanical, including photocopying, recording, or by any information storage and retrieval system, without permission in writing from the copyright owner.

This book was printed in the United States of America.

To order additional copies of this book, contact:
Xlibris Corporation
1-888-795-4274
www.Xlibris.com
Orders@Xlibris.com

38546

Contents

Acknowledgments 7

Am I Lonely 11
Scar tissue 13
It Works for Me! 14
The Impulse To Love Dissected 16
Aisha 17
My Favorite Black Cat 18
The Ultimate Challenge 19
Time 21
New Yorking 22
Love Found and Lost 24
New Beginnings 25
A Favor so Small 26
Holding on 27
Elsie 28
Trust me 29
When Our Love Died 32
Aisha 34
A Sweet Offering 35
To Dream 36
Forbidden Fruit 37
I Worry About You 39
To Micki 41
Reasons 42
About 43
And I Thank You 44
Snake 45
When The Wrong One Loves You Right 47
Happy Birthday Aunt Bettie 48
Where Books Can Take you 49
Aisha 50

Forgive Yourself	51
Go Back to Start	52
Old Lady Blue	53
Thanksgiving Poem	55
Letter to a Friend	56
I Like the City	57
The Bookmobile	58
Senior Moments	59
Fireworks	60
Lyrics for Roy Love Therapy	62
A Graceful Place	64
Two Young Lovers	65
Hero of the Battle	66
4-8-97	68
To my Son Jai	70
Are Tears Really Wasted Water?	71
My Attitude	72
Happiness is?	73
Lucky Stars	74
Wings Cost Money too	75
Minorities	76
A Passion Bizarre	77
Love	79
Life's Circumstances	81
Abduction	82
Short Stuff	84
Old Black Men	85
These are a Few of My Favorite Things	87
My Sweet Georgia Bird	88
Something Broke	89
Marty Died Today	91
Ancient Wino	93
My Sister Cynthia	94
Cheyanne's Blood Tub	97
Star Child	100
Ashes	103
Living in the Aura of Greatness	104
My Autobiography	109

Acknowledgments

Thanks to all those who have shown me love and understanding. I love you back. I have had angels come in and out of my life with every step of my trek. They have appeared to me in several different shapes and dimensions.

L.S who took a second job and helped me and the kids, appeared on the evening when I had no money and the hotel manager refused to allow us to stay just one more night. I knew for certain I would have money the very next day. When he arrived I was in the hotel lobby in Manhattan, holding on to my babies, sobbing but wanting to scream at the thought of yet again riding the trains all night. He rescued us. I've never forgotten your kindness my friend.

Thanks again R.C. who gave me love and affection when my self-esteem was so low I was having a hard time loving myself.

Thanks to the kindhearted case worker at the welfare office who arranged a course for us that would help return our lives to some degree of normalcy.

My 6ft 4in "little brother" Billy. He came back to Brooklyn to get his 5ft 11in "big" sister, his niece and nephew and moved us to Richmond Va. where we had a chance for a "do-over" Thanks, Momma's Baby Boy.

There are nights when my murdered son visits me, shakes my bed and I wake up in a blue funk. Then I think about his four beautiful children: Margaret, Lateshia, Takeshia, Trey (Martin Wayne Scott III). I am so grateful that I can clearly see him in them. Thank you Jai!

I also want to thank my step-son Andre who lived with us for awhile and was murdered when he returned to Newark N.J. Andre shared his sweet spirit with me. I miss you too.

My other step-son Derrick is a gift from God and such a joy to be around. Thanks you, Mom loves you very much.

My daughter Cheri shares her wonderful daughter Cynthia with me on Saturdays. Thank you Cheri. Cynthia's warm smile and bright face always reminds me how good it feels to laugh out loud. Thank you Sunshine Nana will always love you, no matter what.

James, Thanks for finally emerging into the family man I felt you always could be. May we continue to do the work that will strengthen our relationship.

A special thanks is reserved for my daughter Jaime Nicole. Jaime has been my right and left hand in this project. It's amazing to me how this generation becomes computer savvy so quickly. I'm from the typewriter and long-hand era. Today it's computers and disc. Now, I'm still fighting and kicking, trying to embrace all this awesome technology that I find absolutely fantastic and fabulous.

I don't want to give the impression I survived my ordeal unscathed. I continue to be a functioning agoraphobic. I've also been diagnosed with "Delayed Stress Syndrome Disorder". After effective treatment I maintain a life worth living that I believe is blessed with favor and grace.

One of the greatest lessons I've learned is that love is never wasted.

Carol Diana Patterson

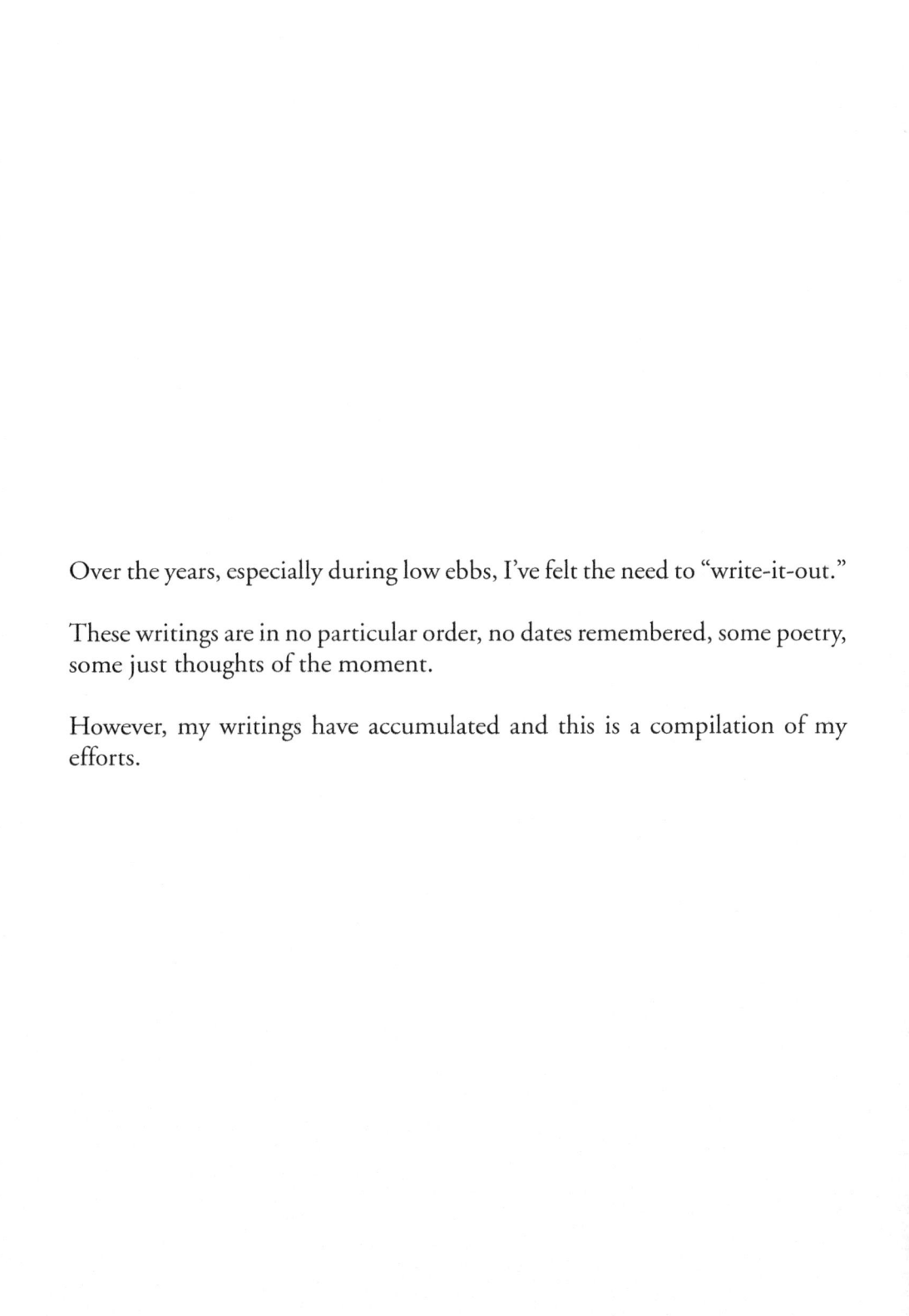

Over the years, especially during low ebbs, I've felt the need to "write-it-out."

These writings are in no particular order, no dates remembered, some poetry, some just thoughts of the moment.

However, my writings have accumulated and this is a compilation of my efforts.

Am I Lonely

Am I Lonely
    Would that explain the pain
Am I Lonely
    What did I hope to gain.

Whatever it was
    It no longer is
The dreams I dreamt
    Were not dreams of his

What changed the course
    We hoped to follow
How did the vision
    Turn so hollow

I miss the togetherness
    We once shared
A time when secrets
    Were so easy to bare

The walks, the laughter
    The learning, The love
A spiritual experience
    A connection to God above

We grew together before
    Apart we grew
The panacea was love
    We thought we knew

Love meant nothing
    When King Heroin intervened
A societal curse ghettos breed
    To me it seemed

He stuck the needle in his
    Veins so deep
When he missed a shot
    With him I'd weep

That time has passed
    Yet the pain won't go
Am I lonely
    If so, for what I don't know

Scar tissue

There's a sadness inside him
    You can sense but can't reach.
He won't let you.

Scar tissue leaves a mark too.

    He won't leave the door ajar
    He won't let you in
    He won't trust himself so far
    He knows how things have been.

Scar tissue leaves a mark too.

    When you find a way to ask him why
    Without adding to what is
    Wetness comes to big brown eyes
    Warming your heart but freezing his.

Scar tissue leaves a mark too.

    His mother says he is her stray
    He says she didn't love him
    His love for her shines anyway
    He knows most times too dim

Scar tissue leaves a mark too.

    You know he will never love you.
    You know he can't let you in.
    You look just like his momma did
    You might take him to places he's been

Scar tissue leaves a mark too.

It Works for Me!

In good relationships we have
An inclination to seek strength
From our partners, right or wrong.

But it's scary when we see
The others' soul crumble
Before our very own eyes.

It's scary when weaknesses
Reveal themselves.

It's scary when you know
You chance rejection after
Every revelation.

Yet it's the other's strength
That can allow us to melt,
To liquefy, to freeze and
Become whole again.

You allow me this. God gives us the strength
We need through Him,
Through each other.

Perhaps I do depend on
Men to contribute to my
Emotional well being
This I don't deny.

It works for me
I'm that kind of woman.
I need the rap, the hug,
The caress. Soothe me.

I guess I can be afforded
These comforts from
Another woman.

The trouble being you can't linger.
You can't savor.
Passionate compassion not
Affected by gender is often misinterpreted.

I am a heterosexual woman.
You are all man.
I find peace in your comforting arms.

You are dependable.
I like that.

It works for me!

The Impulse To Love Dissected

People come and go. They come, share your life, touch your heart, then go. We never know for how long any relationship will exist as it exists. No guarantees! Yet there are those that touch our lives, that impress us, that we don't forget. We may not think about them every waking moment, yet we don't forget them. We don't forget their manner, we don't forget their smile. We remember and warmth spreads throughout our bodies when that kindness which was mutual creeps into our thoughts.

If I were asked to summarize my feelings for these blessed relationships, I would say I felt love. Only now have I decided to examine that impulse. I got out my Funk& Wagnalls to see what they have to say about love.

Love (luv) n.

1—A strong, complex emotions or feeling, causing one to appreciate, delight in, and crave the presence or possession of another and to please or promote the welfare of the other; devoted affection or attachment.

2—Specifically, such feeling between husband and wife or lover and sweetheart.

3—Sexual passion or the gratification of it.

4—A very great interest or fondness: love of learning.

Love is the yearning or outgoing of soul toward something that is regarded as excellent, beautiful or desirable.

AHHHH LOVE!!!

Aisha

I love a little girl
Who brings joy to my world

She's six years old
And a treasure to behold

Her name is Aisha
No one could be sweeter

Her smile, oh how bright
Warms in orange and red light

Loving you is easy, Baby Girl

      Your Laughter
      Puts the Life
    Back in
     MY
       WORLD!!
         MOMMIE

My Favorite Black Cat

My favorite cat is not very fat
My favorite cat is beautiful and black
My favorite cat has a big toy rat
And he likes to play with his rubber bat

My favorite cat likes to chew on my mat
My round green mat where once I sat
My favorite cat has a big black hat
It covers his head from that worrisome gnat

(This poem is a poem that, my daughter,
Aisha and I put together about her cat "Tiger")

The Ultimate Challenge

It looks like I'm working
    Graveyard again
Though I haven't pulled that shift
    Since way back when

I sit here now, it's 5:00 am
    Don't know where I'm going
Know where I've been

My mind is spent, my back is bent
    Yet sleep won't come
    Nowhere to run.

Still trying hard
    To figure out
The scheme of things-
    "What's it all about"

We live, we die
    Yet in between
We tell the story
    Of what our eyes have seen.

Our accounts are filled of joy
    Mostly pain
It's been said by some,
    "No pain-No gain."

Life's trails give us character,
    If we give the waves a ride
Heads up, force a smile
    No ones sees the scars inside.

I feel the sadness
    In every man's eyes,
I sense the hurt in
    Our children's cries

What gets us up to start
    A new day,
What gets us thought times
    That look so grey?

The will to survive
    To fight to the end
Is the ULTIMATE CHALLENGE
    Facing all men.

Jah is watching
    From a place on high
Watching everyone till that
    Time we die

Meanwhile, hold that Brother's hand,
    Touch that sister too
Give each other the strength
    That will pull us all through.

Embrace that young boy.
    Hold on to that girl
We must face the challenge
    Oh, if I ruled the world.

Time

Time present is time past.
What might have been is an
Abstraction . . . a perpetual
                    Possibility . . . .

New Yorking

In a place that's peopled
The odds increased that
You'll find someone
Just one someone
To help you get through
The next quarter mile
Just in the nick of time.

    NY

Where everybody is every age and
Numbers are something you play

    NY

The 2 suitcases I carried were
Stuffed with more blue notes
Than clothes, exit.
I'm gone for me and my two kids.

    NY

Escape-clean
Transition-still.
Am I lonely?
For what, I don't know

    NY

Homesick?
Maybe, but a taste should suffice
To remind me of reasons why
Reasons why I left

    NY

In a place that's peopled
The odds increase that
You'll find someone
Just one someone
To help you get through
The next quarter mile
Just in the nick of time

    NY

Love Found and Lost

I want you to always be part of my life

The part that knows love
The part that causes me to glow
The part that captures my soul
Then allows it to soar.

Let the bridge that distance
Created be shortened
By everlasting memories,

By the vision of your smile
By the dreams of being
With you again . . . .

New Beginnings

The other night I got a call
From Brooklyn-no better place at all.

It was to learn a friend of mine.
Was ecstatic with her recent find.

She found freedom although a price you pay
Is necessary to see the bright of day

It's necessary to feel warm light
Secure, knowing he'll be there through the night

Without the guilt that shadows bring
But with the song that makes hearts sing.

My wish for you and yours holds true
Happy days and few nights that are blue

Good luck my friend in your new home
Good luck my friend with your new love.

A Favor so Small

Was it really too much to ask . . .
A favor so small . . .
After all we've been through . . .

Is the friendship valid
Only when you want it to be . . .

To agree to do
Then change your mind

For selfish reasons
That pierced my heart

Your phone by your side
My phone never rang

Questions with no answers
Or rather answers written in
BOLD RED LETTERS

Or were they green
Jade green or was it jealous green

Our pact in blood turned to water
The steady drip deafening

Was it really too much to ask . . .
A favor so small . . .
After all we've been through . . .

It meant just that much to me
A favor so small!

Holding on

To feel alive what must I do
I've changed in ways that say I'm through

Through with people, through with love
What happened to me and the stuff I'm made of

My strength is gone, I don't know where
If I look too hard, I find only a tear

To protect my self from grief and pain
I exist within these walls
My habits are such I'm destroying myself
Mind body and all

Yet something inside is crying to me
And won't let me rest in destruction
Won't let me bask in the sea of corruption
Won't let me look for abduction

Until I find the nerve to die
Which will forever silence my cry

I must find a way to somehow live
Somehow find strength to give and give

If a caring soul be near as I crawl
An embrace will help to answer my call

If only for a while a reassuring kiss
Will ease the pain, will replace what I miss

IT'S CRAZY THE COMFORT
WE SEEK IN SAD TIMES
CAN PRODUCE A CHILD
WITH SAME ANSWERS TO FIND!

Elsie

Your beautiful sweet/sad
Eyes etched a forever place in my heart!
        I wish you peace and love
              Always
              Carol

(P.S
Elise died 2 years after I wrote this on her 24th birthday card.
A rare stomach cancer they said.
They took her body home to Ethiopia)

Trust me

He said "Trust me!"
I'm what you need
We'll have beautiful children
That I will feed

I'll stand by you
When things get tuff
We'll survive the storms
Our love is enough

To be next to you
Two souls will connect
Said vows will be
Produce provide and protect

I'll ease into you
Long awaited maiden voyage
My heart is young
And full of courage

My love is strong
You are my sweet
My lips are warm
Don't you feel my heat

Sweet vows were said
Till death do us part
I believed in him
With all my heart

As with all life
Things did get tuff
Joy injected with needles
Our love wasn't enough

The love I had
he didn't need
Our two beautiful children
He couldn't feed

After drugs took his mind
Yes, I went my own way
Our two children I fed
If only day by day

Then along comes #2
Look what I found
Love is so good
The 2nd time around

He said "Trust Me!"
I'm what you need
We'll have beautiful children
That I will feed

My love is strong
You are my sweet
My lips are warm
Don't you feel my heat

Sweet vows were said
Till death do us part
I believed in him
With all my heart

As with all life
Things did get tuff
I gave my best
But will love be enough?

As it was once before
His pain I could see
His momma didn't love him
So he took it out on me

My love is strong
You are my sweet
My lips are warm
Don't you feel my heat

No thanks, I'm chilly
I need my sweater
Only God will I trust
He warms me better!!!

When Our Love Died

I gave away your love yesterday
You didn't want it anyway.

I gave away my love yesterday
Raindrops on rooftops, tap rhythms
in a loves way

Sparks ignited, long sleeping passion
Afrocentric movements designed
For serious action

His smile engaged me
And lit up my life
Visions of what it should be
Minus loads of unnecessary strife

I gave away your love yesterday
You didn't want it anyway!

I prayed so long to understand
Why you just would not care
Why you found it so hard
So hard to be fair

Where is your head
Don't you know live is good
Don't you know love taste sweet
If you only would, if you only could

You let me face it alone
Time after time and again
If I'm alone, I'll be alone
Till this broken heart mends

I gave away your love yesterday
You didn't want it anyway
I gave away my love yesterday
You didn't want it anyway!

Aisha

Allow to be aware
Of all the things around you

Allow yourself to have a dream
And the courage to see it through

Allow yourself to sometimes fall
And from that fall you'll learn

Allow yourself to live your life
Blessed with the goodness you've earned

Allow yourself to be attentive
And listen to those who are wise

Allow yourself to be assertive
and keep your eye on the prize!

LOVE
Mommie

A Sweet Offering

The sweetest thing I've ever known
Is longing to be told
To see our kids whose hearts have grown
Is worth more than precious gold

The togetherness, the laughter
The learning, the love
A spiritual experience
We thank you, God from up above

From different worlds, from different places
They came, to strut their stuff
Their glow warmed even the saddest of faces
Their smiles were quite enough

Imperfection, didn't stop them
Everybody is a star
Inspiration, hope will guide them
Makes no difference who you are

A sweet offering they gave.
Our kids did their very best
Precious memories we will savor
Of how they met the test

So we wish you well & many thanks
For Kid's Sake kids far & near
Your T.V. show brought us joy, hope & love
That will last though out the year

We'll place the future in your hands one day
So remember in all you endeavor
Be free to create, to listen, to stay
What I do today, matters forever!!

Aisha's Mom

To Dream

And when I wake
I want to be
The entity my dreams
Allow for me

I want to laugh
I want to sing
My arms out stretched
To embrace each fling

Why is it that
Only in sleep I find
The freedom to pursue
The excursions of my mind

Why is it that
Solely in sleep I dare
To be awake and
Live my life clear of fear

Forbidden Fruit

I took a bite from the fruit
From the tree that's forbidden to me

It was sweet, made me complete
Caused me to see what I could be

One bite, one night, now things
Won't be the same

Two loves too late
Where should I place the blame

Lonely tear, healing tears
Sprinkle the tree that's forbidden to me

The taste of the fruit
That sweet, sweet fruit

Instilled in me
The desire to breathe free

Free to give unconditional love
Free to place your smile way above

Above the dread that fills my heart
Above the knowledge that one day we'll part

My life's been enriched
Though the tree can't be mine

Forbidden fruit, flavored like
Bittersweet heady wine

No matter what, no matter why
I'll forever recall that fruit I tried

I'll savor it's taste
I'll savor it's sweetness

Forbidden fruit
You are my weakness

I Worry About You

I worry about your silence when
You hurt the most and are afraid to cry

I see the way you try so hard
To intellectualize and understand why

You dissect yourself, you look within
You rip your soul apart

I know she was your Onyx Queen
She once captured your lonely heart

For her you did the things one does
The extraordinary things one does for love

You financed her dreams, not knowing one day
Her career would be placed far & above

You ignored the signs your gut could see
You wanted your family complete

Did you find the right words to say
As you watched your daughter's smile deplete

Giving up what you knew to be paradise
Sacrificing what was right for you

Being kind, being selfless, showing compassion
Left nothing for her to do

She used your body, she used your mind
She stripped you naked, right down to the bone

She wiped her soles all over your dream
She used your name 'till she got her own

I worry about you, don't whip yourself
Don't waste your time placing blame

It's over, she's gone, you tried, move on
Good riddance, there is no shame

I worry about you

To Micki

They told me you were absolutely beautiful
I told them somehow I knew that

They told me John's smile lit up the room
I told them somehow I knew that

They told me the look of love between
you and your Dad was unmistakable
I told them somehow I knew that

They told me your wedding day
Was an affair to remember
I told then somehow I knew that

They told me I should have been there
I told them somehow I hope
you knew I was

    Congratulations
      Love
        Aunt Luckie

Reasons

You asked why?
    Why did I trust you?

After all, I'm a loner. I'm a skeptic
    Why did I decide to share me with you?

After all, I'd become selfish with myself.
    I'd become cool like that.
    Why did I choose to open closets
    whose doors had been shut for so long
    and chance losing you,
    when I sensed you would
    be so good for me.

After all, I knew the deal. No one was real!
    You are an exception to the rotten rules.
    You my brother, my lover, have renewed
    my faith in Humankind, at the
    right time. Time becomes a little
    more precious with each grey hair.

You are real

After all, I know the deal
    I choose to feel!

About

About time?
About what?

About achievement
About movement

Necessary to life
Necessary to live

About understanding
About demanding

Necessary to life
Necessary to live

About concentration
About penetration

Necessary to life
Necessary to live

About time?
About what?

About Everything

    All

And I Thank You

I've known a smile that makes me smile
And a laugh that makes the tension float out to sea
    and I thank you

I've known hugs that gave me the freedom to let go
And I know I wouldn't fall
    and I thank you

I've known kisses so gentle that my soul cried real tears
And I was no longer afraid
    and I thank you

I've known the joy of lovemaking so intense that time seemed to suspend
And nothing else mattered
    and I thank you

I've known a tenderness so sweet I felt I could fly
And make a cloud my home
    and I thank you

I've known the kind of friendship that transcends distance
And makes caring a bridge
    and I thank you

I thank you for allowing me to safely experience so many emotions
So many levels of passion
    and so many dreams

Snake

He said, "My name is what I am."
They call me "Snake!"
I'm black, I'm long, I'm beautiful, dreds soft!

When we spoke I saw other lands
I touched other souls
I felt other breath. Life transformed!

He said his people were **Afro-Indian**
And of this he was sure
And of this he was proud. So proud!

He said he always heard music in his head
And of this he was joyous
And with this his heart kept time. Drum beats!

He said being institutionalized was no joke
Depressed, psychopathic, melancholy.
If robbed a man of his soul. Lost soul!

He said the treatments were called "Shock!"
His nerves still quivered with intricate gyrations
His brain, still on fire. Pain ablaze!

He said he knew he was a king
A leader, a chief, important, powerful
He felt it in his bones. Tall regal!

He said he knew God's love
Infinite, good, devoted, just
He felt it in his heart. Shouldn't everybody!

He said why should he be denied love
The love of a woman, the love of a child
Delirious people need love too. Doesn't everybody!

He said my body needs touching
Long-continued drought
My skin is thirsty, Dry parched!

He said let me quench my thirst
Then when I'm full
I'll give it all back to you. Straight shot!

He said be queen to my king
Your pedestal awaits you
Let me give to you. Forever lasting!

He said come melt with me into oneness
Let me love you!
Let me inside. Inside you!

He said then we will die together
Unafraid to leave this cruel world
Free to love. Forever together .

The light from his beautifully wicked hazel eyes, that warmed her being with overpowering desire, suddenly disappeared.
Her fine brown graceful body lost its honey-rich hue& turned chalky grey,
As he squeezed the trigger, first shooting her, then himself.
He lay beside her as their spirits intertwined, ascending pain, ascending life.

When The Wrong One Loves You Right

I want to tell you how much you thrill me.
To see you, to hear your voice
Awakens every sleeping desire to hold you close.
Close enough to hear your heart beat.
Close enough to mesh with the rhythms of your warm body.

Your movements trigger
A response in me that reaches a place known only to you.
Loving you has been my joy.
Loving you helps me to embrace life.

I've learned from you,
I've found comfort in your strong arms.
When you're with me my tender lover,
My insides explode with the sweet electrical eruptions of ecstasy.
Take my love, I'll keep it warm for you.
Take this sweet love.

Happy Birthday Aunt Bettie

Keep having your birthdays
Year after year

Continue to celebrate with
Those you know care

My wish for you is simple
Make sure you have big fun

Enjoy your special day, my aunt
For to me you're second to none!

Where Books Can Take you

Books can take you to many places
Books can put smiles on many faces

Exotic countries, faraway lands
Native costumes, Oriental fans

China, Japan, Africa, Spain
Stay right at home & visit Maine

Learn about people that are different than you
Ride a canoe on waters so blue

Books can take you everywhere
To interesting places far and near

Aisha

A is for Acumen
   which you have plenty of

I is for Isis
   Egyptian Goddess of love

S is for your Spirit
   which gives energy to others

H is for your Humor
   which brings joy to all your brothers

A is for Auspicious
   which is a good way
   to end this song

   I'm glad there's no more
   letters to use, cause then
   this song would be to long

       ~MOM

Forgive Yourself

Whatever mistakes we make along the way
When judgment errors pierce a sunny day

We must put our pain & misery aside
Learn to forgive ourselves, learn to collect our pride

For to go on, we must challenge our minds
And find the best way to leave the pass behind

So we pray for strength to start anew
To begin again to be a better you.

Go Back to Start

Life's trials knock us down
    again and again
We wake up, we get up
    for the day about to begin

There's no way to know
    which way the day will go
There's no way to know
    which way the wind will blow

Sometimes the things we plan
    come about without a hitch
Sometimes the things we plan
    will never make us rich

Yet somehow we'll go on
    live on, pray on
Yet somehow we'll find away
    to keep us flexible, to keep us strong

Old Lady Blue

Leave me alone
As I sit on my couch
With little energy left except to dream,
            except to dream

I'm old and I'm tired
And I'm feeling all of my 90 years
Strange, even the good memories
            are growing dim

My once much talked about
Dark and thick flowing tresses have faded
            faded into yesterday

My hair is white and thin
My eyes are red and blue
How can I make the mirror lie

So if you think my hearing aid doesn't work
Cause I stare at you when you talk
You're dead wrong, dead wrong

Just leave me alone
As I sit on my couch
With little energy left except to dream
            except to dream

In Paris one bright and radiant day
When my world was young
And my smile turned up, not down

Two dashing Frenchmen called out to me
They appreciated my loveliness
They made sure everyone noticed

I wanted to strut my stuff in my elegant way
In my new crisp summer dress
With it's magnificent display of wild flowers

I really felt pretty, I longed to dance the pirouette
But I lowered my eyes, sweet innocent coquette
And I continued to stroll the Champs-Elysées

My talent was given to me by God, you know
Europe & America showcased my drawings and paintings
These old unsteady hands hesitate
to create anything, anymore

So, if you think my hearing aid doesn't work
Cause I stare at you when you talk
you're dead wrong, dead wrong

Just leave me alone
As I sit on my couch
With little energy left
Except to dream . . . young dreams

Thanksgiving Poem

How many times do you
    Stop and wonder

About the universe and
    The sky we're under?

It is!!!
And yet, what makes it be
To walk, to talk, to laugh to see

How many times do you
    Stop and wonder

About the universe and
    The GOD we're under?

He is!!!
Just look at me, at you
Give thanks for all of the things you do!

Letter to a Friend

When your world is dark and your problems are real, and you're powerless to change them, what do you expect from your friends? Do you want your friends to leave you alone? Would you rather solitude to best think it out? Or do you want them to be around & call & say, "Hi. What's new," even though you wonder if they can really feel your pain, even though you know they can't really help.

You work hard, you follow the formula & you want the seeds you so carefully sowed to reap a plentiful harvest. There's been enough rain but not enough sunshine.

Seasons change!

How can I help till they do?

        Sincerely,
        ~C

I Like the City

Stompin' when the need is stomp
Sleepin' when the need is sleep
Rompin' when the need is romp
Peepin' when the need is peep

    &

  Creepin'
    when
      the
        need
          is
            creep

The Bookmobile

Whenever you see the bookmobile
Let me tell you what you should think;
Think about the crew
And the blood, sweat and ink
Think about the weather, the rain, snow & sleet
Think about wondering where you will
Get a bite to eat
Oh No! that one's full of gloom
Now tell me, does it really matter
As long as we use "The Room"
Hurry back, what'll you find
Children wall to wall
All sizes, all shapes
Look at that, some learning how to crawl
Oh well, if you're gotta go
And go you must or stay
Give me the bookmobile
I wouldn't go any other way

Senior Moments

I didn't get it
Now I regret it
Should have listened to what they were saying

When Autumn's leaves go
Winter paints the grass with snow
Must have thought the "Old Folks"
Were playing

Now it's my turn to moan
Now it's my time to groan
My legs don't work like they used to

My back talks to me
Screams, yells, squawks at me
Sometimes I lie and say it's the FLU

There are names I forget
Dates and times I forget
Cousin Karl refers to as "Senior Moments"

Said moments I've had many
Better than not having any
Of this I am strongly adamant

Till I wake up stone dead
Still trying to keep my head
Saying by to my last November

I'll hold tight to the fun times
Try to deal with the sad times
Blessings, Senior Moments, let me remember

Fireworks

What do you do with all the hate
The hate the blankets your soul
And keeps the sun-rays at bay

What do you do with all the hate
The hate that frowns your face
And downs the corners of your smile

Do you search for a place to put the rage
The rage that gives your back a hump
And causes the twitch you wish to hide

Do you search for a place to put the rage
The rage that blinds your eyes
And bows your heavy head

But, we're a people expected to
Deal with the crap
The crap that wants us to
Show up for work
And then find a way to become invisible

But, we're a people expected to
Deal with the crap
The crap that made our ancestors weeps
And drowned them in dreams
Of other lands

So, what do we do with all the hate
So, what do we do with all the rage
So, what do we do with all the crap

Some turn it into love so they can go on
Go on to produce, to provide, to protect
And to teach our young the rewards of grace

Some turn it into unbridled fury
Fury that illuminates the sky with crimson pain
And flood the senses with more hate, more rage

Lyrics for Roy
Love Therapy

I need a little love therapy
I know you'll be so good to me

Sweet sassy eyes that warm your face
The way your hips sway to the rhythm
               of the bass

I need a little love therapy
I know you'll be so good for me

As natural as the wind and summer rain
We'll share loves sweet & wet champagne

Chorus

Can you think of something wild
That would satisfy this child
That would make my lonely heart sing
That would fill me with the joy that love brings

I need a little love therapy
Don't you know you'll be good for me

Intimate dinners at my place
Soft shadows from candle light,
Frame your face

I need a little love therapy
The warmth of your body sizzles
When you touch me

Talk to me, show me you care
Can't think of anyone but you, my dear

Chorus

I need a little love therapy
Let me hold you close to me

Solid gold freak, ounce for ounce
Don't worry 'bout me, I'll never bounce

I need a little love therapy
Hot chocolate dripping down the front of me

Keep your love sweet, whatever you do
Please let this dream of mine come true

Chorus

A Graceful Place

I'm learning to live in a better place
A place that promises laughter & grace

I'm feeling freer, can I maintain this pace
Can I maintain the pace to stay in the race

The rhythm of the drum, keeps a smile on my face
Now, dancing with angels, faith fills my new space

Two Young Lovers

He said he felt the need in me
HE said he knew before I knew
That I would need somebody soon
Need somebody, to make it two

I knew I felt the need in him
To know love's warming fire
To dance upon the face of the moon
In the glow of love's burning desire

His hands were big and beautiful
His arms I could see were strong
Strong enough to hold me firmly
Hold me steady, hold me long

The sound of his voice made me quiver
His bass, traveled up from his toes
The joy of his laughter excited my heart
Painting love's healing balm on my woes

My horizons were yet still in focus
Wild dreams tantalized my young mind
I envisioned a full life worth living
With the right mate I knew I would find

We were drawn together fervently
Just like a spider to a fly
Much too young to comprehend that,
A love like this must surely die

Love like this must surely die you know
Too hot, too sweet, too sad
How to carry on is the trick to show
Too hurt, too blue, too bad

Hero of the Battle

I'm the hero of the battle, baby
No war is too tough for me

If you have a problem, big or small
Jump in your ride & come see me

I'm the hero of the battle, baby
Don't you hang your head down low

I've got mighty strong, shoulders, honey
You can lean on, don't you know

You say you don't want me, but you need me
That's a story I've heard before

You say you don't want me, but you need me yet
You're knock, knocking at my front door

I'm the hero of the battle, baby
Now you know just who to call

Loving like mine don't come often
In my arms are where you'll fall

I'm the hero of the battle, baby
Come watch me do my magic

To go through life without good loving
Nothing could be more tragic

You say you don't want me, but you need me yet
You call me in the midnight hour

You say you don't want me, but you need me
To fill you up with my forceful power

I'm the hero of the battle, baby
I'm what you want and what you need

My heart is yours just don't abuse it
If you'll be kind, I'll let you use it

I'm the hero of the battle, baby
I'll earn my chance & you will see

Your face will smile when you know love
And then your heart will belong to me

4-8-97

What could have happened that night
That frantic night
That brutal night
That crimson night
That night, that ended with the life
    leaving your handsome black body

What could have happened to his mind
To his troubled mind
To his sickened mind
To make him want to shoot you
To kill you, to murder you

Didn't he know you would
Rather talk it out, yell it out
Rather negotiate
Rather walk it out
Rather make peace

Didn't he know you had 4 beautiful children
You wanted to watch become adults
You had a mom and two dads
You had two lovely sisters
You had a family that cared

Didn't he know the pain I would feel
How I cry everyday
How I see you everywhere
How I can't make it real
How I can still feel where he severed the umbilical cord

What kind of monster is this
How dare he steal your life away
How dare he spill your blood
How dare he look so innocent
How dare he take the sun out of our day

Now, I'm suppose to forgive him
To find a way to understand
To show compassion for someone else's son
To care about someone who didn't care about me
To be Christ-like, to show love

Well, I don't quite know how to do that
After all, you are my son
After all, you are my only son
After all, you are my first born
After all, you were absolutely unique

So, I don't know how I'm feeling
I think forgiving is a long way off
I think my tired head aches
I think my heart's pounding too loud
I think I can't think . . . think . . . can't think
I can't, I can't . . .

To my Son Jai

I know it's hard to be a Prince in a land that doesn't recognize your father as King.

Or for me to know in my soul that my essence flows with Queenly aura and I know they know, but fear won't let them recognize.

Know my son, that the brightness of your STAR warmed all of us who loved you. Know that your way of lightening our burdens by sparking us with your contagious humor will never, ever be forgotten.

 Know that your charismatic way of beguiling us with the quickness of your mind, enriched our minds. Know that displaying the formidable strength that made us all feel your regal shoulders were there for us when we needed them, will forever be engraved on our hearts.

Know that I know your journey was short yet long and the path that was given you was interrupted by obstacles that should have been sanded down by those who preceded you.

I recognize you, my son, my prince, and may you finally be able to wear your crown in peace, sweet sweet peace

Love Always!!
Mommie

Are Tears Really Wasted Water?

I cry and I cry and I don't know why
I cry at the sight of the evening sky

I cry at the sound of Mile's blue notes
At the sound of water gently kissing a boat

I cry when a stranger wins, "Let's Make a Deal"
I cry even though a movie's not real

I cry when I think of my son, now gone
At the way only he could enjoy a song

At the way he would fill the whole room with laughter
At the way he always seemed to know what he's after

I cry when I think of my beautiful daughters
So tears must be more than wasted waters

My Attitude

All I have left is my attitude
And that's wearing mighty thin

I've had plenty of this, and a little of that
But it doesn't explain the shape that I'm in.

I have to pretend I want to go on
Yet getting out of bed is a wonder

I've been roughly pushed down, heel piercing my back
Stepped over and left buried under

So all I have left is my attitude
I make noise so they'll think I still care

But I don't, no I won't, must detach, can't see clear
Because, I'm fading away from wear and the tear

Seems, I spent my life helping when I should have let it be.
Now, I know there was much I simply could not see

Some tears were happy, most tears were sad
So I'm left with attitude maybe that's all I've ever had

Happiness is?

I wonder what the size of happiness is
Is it bigger than a bread box
Can it fit in my navy blue shoe
Or is it so small I'll have to magnify it
Or so big, I wouldn't know what to do

I wonder what the color of happiness is
Is it yellow, like huge shiny sunflowers
Can its hue lighten up a room
Or is it dark, like violet blue indigo
Or red, with lots of va-voom

I wonder what the shape of happiness is
Is it round, like it is when the moon is full
Can it sit on top of a piano, edges snug
Or is it a triangle like the pyramids, I love
Or in a square like the living room rug

I wonder what the smell of happiness is
It is fruity, like a cool juicy island mango
Can its aroma change the way that you think
Or is it so stank you must turn away
Or is it so sweet you want to take a drink

I'm not sure that I know, what happiness is
Maybe it's the color of rain when it falls on the orchids
Maybe it smells like the rain when it's fresh and clean
Maybe it feels like the rain when it danced on your head
Maybe it taste like buttery catfish, do you know what I mean?

Lucky Stars

Have you ever been blessed with the time and the space
When the stars are all lined up just right
When the gods are listening to your every word
And the full moon glows so bright

So bright, so right, nothing could go wrong
On a night that cherishes love
So warm, yet cold, lingering snow still around
Kissing the trees, limbs reaching up above

As if to say, as if to pray for this crazy world we're in
My God in heaven, can you hear me tonight
"My child. be at peace, because all is well
When the stars are lines up just right."

Wings Cost Money too

If my cash flow was there
I don't think I would care
I'd hit it and quit it
And take to the air

Don't want to do tangles
Be left to mad dangles
No strings, just good candy
Without any angles

Disappointed and betrayed
My joy's been delayed
Love's great importance
May just be outweighed

Minorities

They call us "minorities"
LIke that's what we are
Colorful people are in abundance
If not here, certainly not far

We populate God's earth
We paint it with style
You know it Mr. White man
We've been here for quite awhile

You call us "minorities"
To mess with our heads
So we'll feel so worthless
We would rather be dead

Psychology will tell you
Negative words cut like a knife
So you use them against us
To add strife to out life

But we're not going to accept it
Your words are hateful and bad
They are designed to cause damage
Lower esteem and make us sad

So a stereotypical slur
In spite of your plan
Will continue to remind us
In time we'll inhabit all this land

A Passion Bizarre

This kind of passion can't be any good
You won't do the things that you know you should

You don't think the world could understand
The kind of loving you get from this man

The way he makes you feel when your day goes wrong
The way he says," For you, I'll be strong"

He protects you, he's gentle, he's just what you need
He makes it so easy to follow his lead

You followed him down a road much too dark
With no light to guide, not even a spark

When the needle was in his arm, you tried to love him less
But compassion kept you there, though leaving him was best

Heroin took over, only the memory of him was there
Yet learned passion kept saying, how could you not care

So you stayed much too long, though it made you so sad
Trying to keep family together, yet he could no longer be dad

The wild passion you once felt, made you think you couldn't live
Without him in your life, your life you'd rather give.

But the pain wouldn't stop, must find a way to go
Must make a better life, no tears, no fears, oh no

Leaving was hard, your family, your love & your mind
Dangerous passion for him, made you leave your heart behind

A lesson well learned, now you know the mistake you made
Loving any man above God, is a love that has to fade.

Love

When I think about love
I think about you
About the trials and tribulations
We've been through

I think about the children and the joys
They've added to our life
A life full of laughter, sprinkled
With our share of strife

When I think about love,
I think about you
About the blessings we've had
That kept our love new

I think about our Lord
His everlasting love
That wraps us in compassion
Light from up above

When I think about love,
I think about you
About how you've enriched my life
Warmed my heart too

I think about heaven
Right here on earth my dear
And my prayer is that
We'll be together year, after year

May God bless our hearts
Let us ride the angels wings
He brought you to me, my love
For this I will always sing!

Put these words in your heart, my dear husband
Know that I love you yesterday, today
And forever more

    Your Wife,
    Velma

(Written for Velma's husband who was in the hospital at the time)

Life's Circumstances

You say the circumstances of
Your birth are suspect to
Say the least
That the man who fathered you
 Is to some a savage raping beast

I'm sure the knowledge of this
Happening makes you sad and
Burdens your soul
Makes you sometimes feel unwanted
makes you feel shame, makes
your blood run cold

And because I wasn't there
That night. There is no way
I would know the deal
But there are some things
I'm learning about
You that I truly believe is real

I believe you have a great
Big heart that you may not
Want everyone to see
I believe you have the patience and
Understanding to be the best
Mom you can be

I believe you are a sweet young
Woman with the courage to
Struggle on
And what ever happened that
Fateful night, I sure am
Glad you were born

(Written for Bonita whose mind stayed troubled because she was told her father raped her mother and she is the product of that union)

Abduction

When I first saw the gun
My instinct was to run
But my heart pounded out fear
The smell of death was in the air

He dragged me to the car
Said it wouldn't be far
It would take only a few hours
To relish his sexual powers

His apartment was clean
Set up like a college dean's
There were rows of books
Everywhere you took a look

The magazines on the stand
The shiny black baby grand
The easel was a study in black and grey
My terrified mind studied how to get away

He sat the gun down
Now his face grew a frown
He ordered me to stand naked before him
Oh Lord, please make the lights dim

He wanted something more
As he threw me to the floor
He arranged me in several a nasty pose
Now, I'm down on all fours, his scent filling my nose

He ejaculated on me, everywhere I could see
He masturbated again and again
If he had plans to stop, I didn't know when

Each time he would come
I wished he were done
I could smell my own fear
Each time he came near

He delighted in sketching
He thought the poses were fetching
An artist by occupation, he said
His works I must have seen
The only thing I could see was
A pink dick deviant sex fiend

I couldn't believe that
He would allow me to flee
I felt so violated I wanted to die
My virgin teenage body all I
Could do was cry
He did let me go, acting like
He wasn't my foe
My brightness was forever tarnished
My defiled brown frame never
Again to be garnished

Never again to feel beautiful
Never again to feel clean
Never again to feel pure
Never again, never

Short Stuff

He was much too short
Society would say
His head stopped
Where my breast began

When we walked together
His hand I would hold

I wanted to protect him
From the on-going traffic
The cars may not have seen him

When we danced
Something seemed right
About me dipping him

When he put his arms
Almost around me
I almost felt hugged

But his kindness won out
And his laughter made me laugh
And he treated me
Like I was his Queen

He was masterful and enlightened and wise
And there were places where our
Sizes didn't matter

Yet, he was much too short
Society would say
And I was much too young
Because I listened, I listened

Old Black Men

There's something about "Old Black Men" that
Warms my heart completely
Their receding hairlines
Encircled in snow-white hair

The way their faces
Tell the story of the struggle
Of just waking up black

To have survived the daily put-downs
Simply based on color
I honor you, I praise you
I pray for you

There is nothing better
Than you sharing your secrets
After all, the young need your focus and guidance

Teach them the hard lessons
You had to learn
Just to be able to go home
At the end of the day

To be able to shelter your family
To feel them, to hug them
I honor you
I praise you
I pray for you

I think about my own handsome
Dark chocolate dad
And the sacrifices
He had to make for us

Tall, regal and proud
Just like he should have been
At the end of his journey
I know God said well done

So, Old Black Men
Receive my love
I honor you
I praise you
I pray for you

These are a Few of My Favorite Things

Street lights that glow
As we play hide and seek
Lovers embracing as we sneak a peek

Beautiful flowers blooming in spring
These are a few of my favorite things

Kittens and puppies full of great glee
A sky so clear as far as you can see

Fierce jamming music that makes me wanna sing
These are a few of my favorite thing

Twirling and dancing till its time to go home
Outfits still slamming 'cause we're bad to the bone

My first grown-up kiss, made me feel I had wings
These are a few of my favorite things

Not that I'm seasoned and quite a bit older
With pains in my back and disc ruptured in my shoulder

It's my children and grands, what pleasure they bring
These truly are a few of my favorite things.

My Sweet Georgia Bird

She came into my life and lit it up
At a time when I needed a spark
It didn't dawn on me that this
Meeting was far from a lark.

She kept popping up
Like a perfectly brown piece of toast
Her personality was brighter and
More engaging than most

Her sunny disposition influences
All that would dear
Dear to hear, dear to come near

We worked together, solved problems together
Been insightful together but oh
The best times are when we go deep down
Pull up laughter that will chase away the woe

Can I be so lucky, be so blessed
To have this beautiful bird
Fly into my nest

Thanks" Sweetness" for including me in your life
For your grace, your charm
Your strength, even in strife

Remember good things can only happen
If you take it day by day
And fill your heart with words
Like delight, prosperity, and blithe
To chase the blues away

My "Sweet Georgia Bird,"
Tressa is her name
Flew into my stormy life
Nothing has been the same.

Something Broke

When my beautiful Mom first held her tight
It was clear her granddaughter would light up the night

Mom gazed into her eyes and a prediction was born
This first Ms Black America will light up the morn

My Cherelle Denise, My Cheri Amore
Little angel girl we all hoped for

Wrapped in promise, wrapped in love
Gentle as a kitten, peaceful as a dove

When my parents met their appointment with God
Life wasn't easy, in fact it was hard

Cheri and her brother Jai gave me reason to always pray
So that someday, somehow we would see a brighter day

After years of struggle, after years of pain
Their Dad, and his addiction, nearly drove me insane

We had to leave town, New York swallowed their Dad
A new life, a new town, afforded a life we never had

We did pretty darn good, as life went on
Nothing is perfect, but homelessness was gone

The kids decided going to New York was good
They experienced hard knocks, like I knew they would

But they stuck it out, wanting to stay with their Dad
needless to say, their decision made me sad

Years went by before they came back
Having learned to do crimes, I know for a fact

They knew how to pillage, they knew how to steal
Their Dad's life of crime was for sure the real deal

For whatever reasons, they did return home
To have changed forever, always eager to roam

My Cheri Amore, I no longer knew
Her sweet demeanor, shown only too few

Something broke never to mend
Our relationship now was only to bend

Jai joined the Army which did him much good
He cared for his family like he knew he should

Cheri's daughter Cynthia, to us a beauty born
Captured our hearts, before our relationship was torn

Now despite the struggle to keep my kids alive
No appreciation, still they did thrive

Time spent, Jai and their Dad Now have passed on
Cheri's still here but exploding with scorn

Something broke and I'm not sure why
God knows I did work hard to try

Nothing left but prayer for my girls
And I still wish for them the best of all worlds

Marty Died Today

Heaven will never be the same.
As one of God's favorite children
I know Miles will be softly blowing the trumpet for him
Ray will be singing soulfully
Paul Chambers will be caressing his bass
The welcoming sound will be like no other.

Here he comes my Lord
His shoulders are bent
His body is worn
His legs no longer work
His laughter has diminished
His smile has faded

What a journey it's been
What a rough road he traveled
What a strange path he chose
His love affair with heroin
Led to AIDS
This unforgiving illness
Led to death

My Lord hear me out
This soul, this gentle soul fought his fight
Valiantly stood his ground and did it his way
When he knocks on your door
Please have our beautiful son greet him
With his arms surrounding him
Whisper in his ear
He's home now and you will take care of them

What a mighty thing love is.
It comforts and endures
My Lord, show him what unconditional love is
He will finally find the peace only you can give

It's over Marty!
I'll carry your wonderful spirit
In my soul
Praying that you will dance again

Put your head up
Spread your wings
Soar my love
Heaven is waiting

Ancient Wino

He sat there with his skinny left leg crossed over his right. His wine bottle was poorly concealed by a while plastic bag he probably got from the corner store. He talked to his imaginary friends. His hands were in perpetual motion, and the light had gone out of his grey-blue eyes years ago, when he still had hair. Watching him you knew his eyes were smiling anyway.

He sat alone enjoying his friend, his family that had forgotten him long ago, and his wine. He was seeing what no one else could see. he was hearing what no one else could hear, what was his life story? Was his youth filled with love? When did he stop loving himself? Did he have children, grandchildren? Did he have a wife who cried and prayed for him? Why did he give up? Why did he?

There but for the grace of God . . . .

My Sister Cynthia

My sister Cynthia was six years older and eight inches shorter than me.
I knew she was different, but the reasons why were slow to see.

Her condition was a topic left unsaid, hush hush you better not ask
Anyway RETARDATION is a word full of shame, you deal with wearing a mask.

Even though I was younger, the responsibilities were always mine
I didn't understand why they called on ME most of the time

It was hard for her to make true friends and do what was right
Her homework was such a chore at times, she struggled way into the night

She wouldn't ride and elevator, an escalator scared her too
To take her to the Dentist and the Dr. was a job you didn't want to do

She would always kick the Dentist, we had to forcefully hold her down.
She didn't want the Dr. to touch her here or there, her extreme fear was in her sound

The bad kids chased her home from school every single day
She was bullied and beat and they made fun of her in every way

I fought her fights, my parents gave me the job and that job was to protect
Coming to her rescue trying to make the situation correct

I did my best to keep her safe, mom and dad knew I would
If only my questions were finally answered then my task would be understood

We shared a bedroom every night, which was so very hard to do
I wanted to escape with the birds, when down south I knew they flew

Cynthia's libido was extremely rich and bursting to overflow
I'd awake to her sounds of ecstasy, faithfully sure to blow

She would pleasure herself right in front of me
Fingers searching for joy, wanting me to see

I thought it was rude, I thought it was sick, I thought it was just plain nasty
Later I realized what it had to be, she had discovered a release with her very own key

The things we had in common were few, we both loved to dance and sing
Music was a constant comfort for her, Jackie Wilson her very own king

I was cool with The Platters, Marvin, Miles and James Brown
Things were always so much better when music was around

There were times when she wrapped herself in hate, successful in making Mom mad
She would call her girlfriends on the phone, explicit sex talk made Mom sad

She said she liked men but she liked women too, it really didn't matter which one
They both made her feel oh so good, she was satisfied when both were done

I managed to accept her and her quirks, then finally the secret was told
She was born prematurely her brain was affected, which made her appear so cold

She stumbled through her life and she did quite well
She held on to her job which at times was pure hell

Well she found it ain't easy to exist in this world
But she knew love, she knew pain, my momma's first baby girl

She shared a secret only to me one day
Uncle Noel told her he wanted to play

He would take her to the playground when it was finally dark
All she knew was they were gonna have fun in the park

He molested her and raped her again and again
She wanted it to stop but she didn't know when

He threatened her and scared her, she was too afraid to tell
He put his big hands over her mouth, when she would try to yell

When she felt safe enough to tell me, she just couldn't take anymore
She cried and her body trembled, she said her "privates" were sore

We knew he starting hurting her when she was still very small
Her instincts somehow told her, she was up against the wall

My job once again was to serve and protect
Now how do I make this situation correct?

I told on the creep, I told and I told, but they didn't want to believe what I said
Another family secret to sweep under the rug, there were times she wished she were dead

He finally stopped, although now he had too, I hated him from that point on
You get to be innocent, to be pure only once, thanks to him her hymen was gone

Cynthia Jr., is in God's heaven somewhere dancing with Jackie now
Getting all the attention from Mom and Dad, well practiced, she knew just how

Cheyanne's Blood Tub

It was so common to open the daily newspaper and see another young girl had been found dead in the alley, the park or by the front door of the hospital, dumped. It wasn't news really. Quacks performed abortions all the time. Not all were successful. This was the time before abortions were legal. Girls and woman were butchered around the clock. Cheyanne's best friend had died after going through an abortion The funeral was so sad. What a senseless death. Cheyanne's little sister couldn't understand. Cheyanne's Mother wondered way it had to be this way.

Cheyanne had a dynamite personality, they all agreed. She was a good girl and one day she would fall in love and marry. They all knew she would be the best mother, her life would have been perfect. She got pregnant, just 20 yrs. old, finished High School with honors and was attending the local university, but she was not married. She really didn't mind being "knocked up", after all she was in love with her fella and he was in love with her. In her mind, they would get married and live happily forever after. Isn't that what the fairy tales promised?

She still lived at home and when she and her fella told her parents, their reaction shocked the couple, although it shouldn't have. Her family was outraged, embarrassed and ashamed, after all Cheyanne was supposed to stay a virgin until she married. She was a good girl, she shouldn't have become pregnant. As soon as she told them, the activity around her made her nervous. She couldn't understand what was happening.

Her dad went upstairs and came back with a fist full of dollars. Her mom looked in her top drawer and found a piece of scrap paper with a telephone number. She heard her mom make an appointment. It was with a nurse's aide that worked full time at a hospital and part time performing abortions. Cheyanne was told to forget about marriage, and about having this baby. Her parents were very vocal about their disapproval.

"You will not disgrace this family! After all, what would the neighbors say. You will abort this fetus. No questions asked whether you like it or not. You live here and we make the rules!"

She was terrified. The date was in three days. She had constant nightmares of her baby boy wrapped around her throat, still attached to the umbilical cord. The cord must have been six feet long and wrapped around and around her neck, strangling her.

When the day arrived Cheyanne had a hard time getting out of bed. She had a hard time getting dressed. She had a hard time washing up. She had a hard time brushing her teeth and her hair. It was morning but what a long day it had been already. She and her mom got on the "A" train and left Brooklyn to go to Harlem, 116th st. They walked up two flights of steps in the apt. A full-figured middle aged brown skinned woman opened the door with a smile. She welcomed them. The conversation between her mom and this woman was nothing more than small talk and light banter.

Her apartment walls were covered in Jesus pictures. The last supper was depicted in the largest framed print. The woman extended her hand to Cheyanne and led her to the bathroom. Her instructions were to strip naked and get inside the tub. She did. The tub was full of warm water. She watched as the woman straightened out a wire hanger. The hanger was inserted inside a long rust colored rubber tube. The woman, who had a smile on her face and Jesus pictures on her walls, tried to make Cheyanne relax. "Lie back and hold your breath, sweetie." "This will be over before you know it, darling." Cheyanne did what she said, tears quietly cascading down her cheeks. She couldn't find any words to say. She uttered, "O.K" She thought of her dead friend, Bernice. Why hadn't she stood up to her parents. Oh, that's right. She still lived at home. She had no money of her own. And during those days a decent girl didn't leave home and live alone. She had to be married. Well, that was out.

Cheyanne held her breath. The woman held the wire hanger in her rubber gloved hand. "Open your legs and put your knees up toward your chest, sweetheart." She plunged the wire hanger deep into her vagina. She moaned in pain. She cried in pain. She screamed in pain. A pain unlike any she has ever known. The tub rapidly filled up with blood. Water and blood. Her blood. The woman told her to wash and dress. The aborted fetus would come out in the toilet at home. The cramps will let you know when it is time. The train ride home took longer than it did to get to 116th St. Cheyanne bled all the way home. Her stomach in knots. She looked up at her mom, expecting just a little bit of sympathy. Her mother looked at her and said "When you make your bed hard, you have to sleep in it lumps and all". That was the last thing she needed to hear . She hated her mother.

When they finally reached home, it didn't take long before the cramps intensified and she sat on the toilet and passed the fetus. She turned around to see it. Blood clots. Blood tissue. Blood everywhere. Nothing that resembled a fetus. She thought of a prayer and said goodbye to her baby. Cheyanne wasn't able to recover. She writhed in excruciating pain. She could do nothing . She begged her mother to take her to the hospital. That was the last thing her mom wanted to do. After all, what would the neighbors think. Cheyanne didn't get better. She was in the hospital for two weeks fighting for her life. She had a serious infection. Her mom didn't tell the doctors why. Cheyanne was sure they knew. She was in intensive care and it looked like she would die. Another wire hanger abortion. It really wasn't news. She pulled through, heartbroken but alive. Her fella visited with her in the hospital. They held each other and sobbed tenderly.

Cheyanne wondered if she would ever be able to have a baby in the future. After all, One of the common results of a botched abortion was that your insides were so seriously damaged, more often than not; you will never be able to have children. You will never be able to be a real woman. After all, woman had the babies. To give your love the precious gift of a child was only natural. Cheyanne's fella enveloped her in his strong arms and never let her go. He loved her, she knew, but will she ever be able to love herself.

Star Child

She watched as he walked into the crowded room. His presence so dominated, that it affected her before she realized it. She felt her own being warming ever so gently, ever so sweetly, as though heated maple syrup was being dripped on to her head and cascading down, down into secret places.

She put her head down and smiled to herself. Embarrassed, as though all those around her somehow knew what she had felt at the mere sight of this man. This tall, magnificent, man.

She slowly raised her head and noticed that most of the people there were adorned in their party attire. He wore fitted jeans and a bright yellow "T-shirt" that simply spelled out the words "STAR CHILD" on the back.

How appropriate, she thought, for this gorgeous body looked liked he had been blessed by the gods. Step back Adonis, and let this beautiful black man show you how it's done!

Although Tony was his name, from that night on when she closed her eyes, the image of STAR CHILD was sketched on her inner lids.

When they met again she felt the familiar warming that gave her body the fluidity to stand tall and feel alive again.

This time he chose her to talk to, to dance with, to share with. She was surprised to find his nature so affectionate. They connected in conversation in a way she had been longing for. Intelligent, warm, humorous. She enjoyed their time together.

When they parted, she looked to the heavens and thanked the gods for gracing her with someone she knew would be a forever friend. She had no doubts. She had experienced the kind of bonding that brings with it incredible peace.

She thought about him consistently. Because his job took him out of town, weekly, he would come and scoop her up, take her to the next county where they would be free to enjoy each other in every way possible.

He had a way about him and the kind of loving which she referred to as "the lasting kind" at least until the next time. Their love was mutual. Their love was sweet. Their love was understanding.

A month went by. She hadn't heard from him. The nightly calls didn't come. Nothing, not a word. Missing him, she found herself wondering if she would ever hear from him again, ever see him again.

They had created such vivid memories; she replayed their encounters over and over again, and felt comforted.

The next time she heard his voice, he was calling her from the hospital. She listened as he told her about the pain, the excruciating pain that held his body captive. The doctors had finally completed the testing and he was having a terrible time dealing with the diagnostic results: CANCER. CANCER... The word itself weakened her and left her body cold, cold with the knowledge of the inevitable suffering her "Star Child' would have to endure. Her mother died with cancer. Flashbacks... Flashbacks to when she was in her very early twenties, she watched her mother face what would be her life ending at the young age of forty-eight. Tony was not yet thirty years old.

Their lovemaking took on a form of tender urgency that would make the angels blush. Already passionate, her "Star Child' almost frightened her with the all consuming desire to be inside her. He would hold her face in his hands making certain their soulful eyes connected and tell her of the incredible comfort he found when their bodies melted together and their burdens seemed to disappear. The warmth of her soft body enveloped him and transported him to where he knew was heaven. She let him take her and she gave him all the love she was capable of giving. She never wanted anyone more. They cried together, they laughed together, they love together. A forever love.

Again time elapsed. He didn't call she couldn't help but be overly concerned. She left message after message. No response. His sister called, and she found out that Tony was dying. Her tender "Star Child' was experiencing an excruciatingly anguished finale. His sight loss, his confusion, his sudden moments of infectious terror, then his final acceptance of death.

A feeling of overwhelming sadness wrapped itself around her and enveloped her frozen body. Sorrow, deep, deepest agonizing sorrow.

Another piece of her heart . . . gone . . . four tragic loses in as many years . . . gone . . . ashes in the eye of the storm, blowing in the grey winds of death.

Ashes

Ashes to ashes and dust to dust
Who said life was sweet
Who said you should trust

Ashes to ashes and dust to dust
If life can't be sweet
Why can't it be just

Lord, how she loved her "Star Child."

And when her world rains
And the thunder deafens her thoughts
And the lightening is aimed at her heart

She finds him in love's rainbow
And she deals with her loses
As she deals with her gain!

Living in the Aura of Greatness

When I look back over my life, I am delighted to recall the times when people who have been touched by God's hands have crossed my path.

1. My family's three story house on Lafayette Ave. was well kept and furnished beautifully. My parents Bill and Cynthia made sure of that. Mom was for the most part a stay at home mom. She was epileptic and it was hard for her to hold on to a job. Dad worked for the N.Y. Transit Authority since the day I was born. He felt my Mom's pregnancy bestowed upon him the blessing of finally having a job that allowed him to care of his family. That's the reason he gave me the nickname of "Luckie." He felt that I brought him good luck in the war time of 1941. When so many white men went to war, it left openings in many important jobs that could now be filled by black men. He would tell us stories about the prejudice he had to deal with just to keep a job. The older I became the more I appreciated my parents and what they experienced. They were born black in a society that through it was alright to enslave Africans so they could become rich using and abusing free labor. When you think about the stories you've grown up with reliving the trials of your parents and your African and Native American ancestry, you're forever left wondering about man's inhumanity to other men. I know now just how great my parents were.

2. Summer camp played a very important role in my life. Every August, since the time I was six years old. I was on a bus that left Harlem, filled with many other inner city kids, going to camp. We were the fortunate ones that had a chance to escape, if only for a while, from the gangs, crime and drug infested ghetto neighborhoods.

3. Diahann Carroll glided across the rocky dirt road as though she had wings. She wore a canary yellow dress with a bellowing skirt that I'm sure draped many crinoline underskirts that were popular in the 1950's. Since this was Camp Miniskink in Port Jervis N.Y., it was highly unusual to see anyone walking in high high heels. The beautiful Ms. Carroll walked the dirt roads as if it were a red carpet. Ms. Carroll, a famous actress at the time, was there visiting her sister Lydia, who stayed in one of the many wooden cabins that occupied the vast land that was Camp Minisink. I was her sister's camp counselor. The campers called me "Luckie." And boy did I feel lucky to be at that site, at that moment to be able to be so close to greatness.

4. It was also at camp that we met Lorraine Hansberry, author of the famous play and later movie "A Raisin in the Sun," the first play written by a black woman to be produced on Broadway in 1959. Diana Sands, brilliantly played the afro-centric young sister whose dream was to become a doctor. They shared with us their fascinating oral history. We were thrilled to be in the presence of these two beautiful, smart and positive woman who allowed us to dream. Recently in 2004, the play was produced yet again and starred Sean Combs, Audra McDonald, Phylicia Rashad and Sanaa Lathan.

5. Because of Camp Minisink's city activities, we had the pleasure of meeting the dancing Hines family: Dad, Maurice and Gregory at the Savoy Ballroom in N.Y. It was in the 1950's and I had my first crush on Gregory. At the time I was taking tap and ballet lessons. Yes, my parents kept me busy. It was the best way to make sure that my sister, brother, and I stayed out of the "streets." Watching the Hines brothers tap was amazing. They were quite young at the time and I was frozen in amazement witnessing their talent. I have loved Gregory all my life and have been thrilled with his success. He could sing, dance and act. I think they call that a "triple threat." He had the goods. I didn't know he had been sick and when he died in August, 2003, my heart broke once again. Miss you baby. You fascinated me with your playful rhythms and your fiery passion for dance.

6. In the 40's I remember meeting Earl Graves, the founder and publisher of Black Enterprise magazine. He too grew up in Bedford Stuyvesant. The magazine was his dream realized. It made me feel real good for this Brooklyn brother. Earl Graves served as an administrative assistant to Senator Robert F. Kennedy. He has gone on to many more admirable accomplishments that have benefited the African American business men and his greater community. Greatness!

7. I finally got out of "Bed-Stuy," Brooklyn, N.Y. with the help of my brother Billy. I moved to Richmond, V.A. with my two small children, Martin Jr. and Cherelle. When we left I was only able to bring two suitcases. When I arrived in Richmond, I realized that only one suitcase had clothes for the 3 of us, the other had pictures of my family including my immediate family. At the time I was so upset that we didn't have more clothes. Since I was never able to retrieve any more of our material things, now I am so very glad that I have these priceless pictures of my family and old friends. My husband's heroin addiction ran us out of Brooklyn. We literally had to start over from scratch.

Billy graduated from AT&T in N.C., the same college that civil rights activist and minister, Jesse Jackson attended. Billy and his family moved to Richmond after graduation. Billy became the Executive Director of the Richmond Redevelopment and Housing Association. He introduced me to Curly Neil of the world famous "Harlem Globetrotters". It was then that I was made aware that beautiful and bald can be used in the same sentence.

8. In Richmond I held many positions and my favorite was when I was a librarian secretary for the Richmond Public Library Bookmobile. It was there that I met a bright ray of sunshine, Norma Jean Blalock. Norma, a teenager at the time, worked part-time and was finishing her senior year in high school. Norma whose energy and smile were infectious graduated from Howard University to become a television producer, radio and T.V. talent and a film producer. She was my friend, my little sister, and my shinning star. When Norma became seriously ill and died way too soon, I knew I had been touched by an angel. I miss her, I miss her, I miss her. We laughed and cried together in a way that only buddies did.

Norma called me one evening and wanted me to come over to her house to meet a friend of hers. Max Robinson, first Afro-American T.V. anchor was sitting in her living room. What an exciting moment that was! Max and I became fast friends, in fact that night he decided that I would be his sister and he my brother. After that meeting I spend many evenings at his home listening to the extraordinary experiences he lived. Max, never really felt comfortable with the fact that he was in the same room with U.S. Presidents, Vice Presidents, global dignitaries, and famous movie stars. He revealed that one or two, or three drinks gave him the liquid courage to deal with his success. His demons got the best of him. He called me one afternoon from a Chicago Hotel, severely depresses and suicidal. It was a desperate call for help. I'm sure it was God that gave me the right words to say to him.

Max wanted to end it all and jump from the balcony. I too, at one time in my life, trying to deal with my parents dying five months apart, a heroin addicted husband, homelessness with two small children to keep alive and fed, all at twenty two years of age was able to relate to his feelings of hopelessness. I talked him down. He cried thankful tears and was then able to rest his body and his mind. When he returned to his home in V.A. I drove him to the doctor and was with him when he was diagnosed with AIDS. I think he knew before then. Norma and I visited Max in a Chicago Hospital when we were asked to leave his room because Oprah Winfrey was there to see him. No, I didn't have the pleasure of meeting her but that was close. Randall Robinson, Trans-African organizer and Max's brother was at the Howard University Hospital where I met him and His beautiful wife while visiting Max. Max didn't life very long after that. I will always be thankful for the chance to know him, demons and all.

9. When I met Miles Davis at a press conference that Norma invited me to, I figured if St. Peter called me after that meeting I'd be ready to go. When I had the opportunity to ask Miles a question, my question was, "Who would he collaborate with musically if he had the chance." I was pleasantly surprised to hear that it would be James Brown. Miles Davis, world famous trumpet master graciously gave me his autograph and consented to taking a picture with his arm around me. My God! This was quite a feat because Miles was known for his sometimes difficult personality. I credit Miles and Marvin Gaye with being the soundtrack to my life during some of the hardest years you can imagine. They literally keep me going.

Music has always played a very important part in my life. I studied classical piano when I was young. I even auditioned at Carnegie Hall and played in a concert there. I like to say before the Beatles played there, my attempt at a little humor. I was pretty darn good if I must say so myself. Unlike a special few I wasn't given the gift to be able to sit down in front of my beautiful spinet piano and play "by ear," without practice. So, practice I did! I practiced and practiced until I was good enough to play the Brooklyn Academy of Music and of course Carnegie Hall. Not bad for a teenager from Bed-Stuy, which at the time was called the largest "ghetto" in Brooklyn, N.Y. Many people refer to growing up in Bed—Stuy as growing up in the streets. I grew up in a loving home with my Mommy Cynthia, My Daddy William, older sister Cynthia and younger brother Billy, not in the streets!

10. There have been so many times in my roller coaster life where my self-esteem has been trampled on by ten thousand horses. I have turned the pages of my life back and have drawn from the wonderful times when my life has been touched by greatness and it has afforded me hope in the most dire of circumstances. I'm living in the aura of greatness!

My Autobiography

If this is being read, it may mean that I have come to the end of my journey. Like the old sweet song says I hope "He'll understand and say well done." What a life it has been! A life filled with the ups and downs that saturate all lives.

I was born in the "ghetto" of Bedford-Stuyvesant, in Brooklyn, N.Y., Kings County Hospital. I was given my nickname while my Mom Cynthia was still carrying me. My Dad William "Big Bill", felt that this pregnancy and this child to come had brought him good luck. So my nickname has been "Luckie", ever since. I do believe they were hoping for a baby boy, as I was the second child. My given name is Carol Diana Simkins. I never felt like a "Carol" what ever that means. When my parents told me they almost named me after my maternal Grandmother "Gertrude", Carol sounded pretty good. Sorry Nana.

My sister Cynthia, brother Billy and I were kept quite busy with social activities to divert our attention from the gang culture that surrounded us. I studied dance, which included ballet, tap and modern jazz. They wanted to put these long legs to good use. I also studied classical Piano and had the incredible experience of performing at The Brooklyn Academy of Music and at the famed Carnegie Hall in Manhattan, N.Y. Now that's pretty special if I must say so myself. Not bad for a brown-skinned girl from Bed-Stuy.

My young life was good and yet tumultuous. My Mom was hit on the head when the kitchen cabinets fell on her one Sunday morning while fixing breakfast for the five of us. Little Cynthia, my older sister and Billy my younger brother and I were playing with our Dad, washing his back while he was in the tub. I was five yrs. old and this is my earliest memory. We were having such a good time playing with Daddy, laughing, when we heard this extremely loud noise and my Mom screaming at the top of her lungs. The image of my Dad getting out of the tub covered with soapy water, running naked and barefoot, stepping on all the broken glass and wood to get to Mommy is forever etched in my mind. What a horrific sight. Screams everywhere, blood everywhere. Pandemonium!

My Mom was an Epileptic from that point on. She would fall out anywhere with frightening seizures that would fill me with terror. There were so many incidences and I'll mention three catastrophic seizures here:

I came home from Junior High School 85, to find her on the floor by the ironing board with the iron burning an impression in her thigh. The smell of her flesh burning sickened me and filled the air. When she died of stomach cancer at 48 yrs. old she still had the entire shape of an iron burned and branded into her thigh. It took forever to heal.

Mommy had a seizure while she sat on the toilet. She fell in such a way that my brother and I had to somehow find a way to get her up. One leg was twisted around the commode, the other around the sink. The bathroom was small and we would never figure out how she managed to get herself in that position. Her head was bleeding where she hit it on a pipe as she fell. We finally got her up with the help of our friends. Her state of undress was an embarrassment to her, to us, and to our teenage buddies.

In those days, the 1940's, and 50's., most people were uncomfortable understanding Epilepsy. Some even felt that those afflicted were somehow demon possessed. We knew better. Because Mom had no memory of the seizure, she was still a very outgoing, gutsy and spirited woman. She had a hard time holding on to a job because when they found out about her illness, she was asked to leave for her safety and theirs. I always worried about her more than she worried about herself. When we couldn't stop her from going to certain events, I would call ahead to tell the people about her condition and how to treat her when or if she had a seizure. Most of the time if she was given water and a cold cloth for her head, it would stop her from having a full blown attack. The trick was to hear the sound she would make just before a seizure and treat her. I don't know why that worked but it did. I lived with the constant fear that I wouldn't be able to get to her in time when she made her telling sounds. When my Dad who was a N.Y.C. train engineer worked the night shifts I became a light sleeper so that perhaps I would hear her and be able to come to her aid. Somehow it became my responsibility.

Although it was a terrible time there were times when we dealt with it with laughter. An example is when Mom would come out of a seizure and ask us what she had been doing, Billy would always say she was about to give him some money. Laughter can help you deal with the tension.

Excitement was in the air. I was dressed in a pretty white dress. My white anklets and white patent-leather shoes complimented my outfit. Mom called a Yellow Cab and off the two of us went toward The Brooklyn Academy of Music. I was to play Chopin at a piano concert. Mom made her telling noise while in the cab. I asked the cabbie to pull over and stop so that I could go to the restaurant to get some water for my Mom. He pulled over, I got out and ran to the restaurant which was right across the street. When I came out with the water, they were gone. In my excitement I must not have made my intentions clear enough. I panicked. This was 1952 and my eleven year old mind just didn't know what to do. My Mom's best friend, Aunt Dottie, lived about 6 city blocks away. I ran screaming and crying all the way. By the time I arrived I had one shoe on and my white socks were no longer white and they were full of holes. Aunt Dottie left a message for my Dad at his job. She called the police and the hospitals and The Academy. We couldn't find her. About 20 minutes later Mom calls wondering where I was. She was at The Academy of Music, not understanding what happened to me. She had no memory of the attack and she was worried about me. Whew! There were so very many scary situations but these three give a glimpse into the life of an epileptic and those who care for her.

There was a time when we could walk the neighborhood without fear. Things changed. The gangs took over the blocks marking their "territory", and things were never the same. They had names like "The Eldorados" and "The Chaplains". We lived on Lafayette Ave. between Thompkins and Troop, Chaplain Territory. My families 3 story brownstone home was well kept and furnished. Dad kept his little patch of green "lawn", well manicured and his morning glories covered the fence in the back yard. He was a gentleman of great pride.

After the violence strangled our neighborhoods the drugs soon followed. It may have been the other way around, I'm not so sure. We had always side stepped broken glass from wine and beer bottles, but now we dodged hypodermic needles and little glassine bags. The corners where we would gather and harmonize "Doo-Wop", were polluted by Winos, Drunks and Heroin addicts who leaned but never fell down.

Most of us couldn't wait to grow up and be able to leave the dangers of Bed-Stuy. The fun times were quickly disappearing. I attended Brooklyn College, right after graduating from Midwood High School in Flatbush. Marty, my childhood friend, my protector, my lust, my love was soon becoming the center of my universe. We eventually married after I became happily pregnant. I wanted nothing more than to have his baby. Although I was 21, we were much too young to marry. But that's what happens when you think you're "grown", and ready . . . We left for Bloomfield, Conn. on our wedding night. Marty and his uncle Harold owned an auto service, gas station shop. Both Jai and Cheri were born in Conn. Our 2 beautiful babies. The kids were 13 months apart and boy did we have our hands full. We enjoyed being parents. We ended up leaving Conn. and moving to North Babylon, Long Island. Marty's mother had always promised him a house when he married. When we accepted the house, we virtually agreed to live in hell. The deal as told to us was that we would help raise Marty's younger sister, Marsha. Marsha was at least 5 years Marty's junior. I had loved Marsha for a while already. Marty's family also lived on Lafayette Ave. directly across the street from us. So the arrangement was fine with us. My mother-in-law who I idolized as a teenager, made our life a living hell. She was so beautiful and well dressed, I wanted to be like her when I grew up. How many times have I heard "You can't judge a book by its cover." She came to visit and stayed.

My last night living in the house in L.I., was ended with Marty's mom putting me and our 2 small children out in the street. She told me that Marty wanted to kill her, and the only way she could rid herself of her son was to make me leave and he would follow. After I left she told Marty he could stay. Ain't that a bitch! When Marty found out about her plot he also left her and her house to be with me and the kids.

At one point we owned a record shop on Sumner Ave. in Brooklyn. Being a music lover I was at my happiest. The mafia wanted to use the store as a cover up for drug distribution. We resisted and Marty ended up brutalized and pistol whipped. He left the hospital with his jaw wired and on crutches. He reluctantly succumbed, started selling drugs, and in a very short time became a mainline heroin addict. I thought I had known hell before but this chapter of my life was incredulous.

Marty sold and used. I was made to cut and bag heroin while we were locked in an apt. with armed guards at the door. They stayed posted until the operation was completed. At that point the 10 of us were body searched and let go. In those days there was an actual person that tested the drugs. Marty and another addict were in the corner of the room testing the consistency of the heroin. The cut had to be acceptable to the buyers. While most of us sat at the table busy bagging, Marty was happily testing the product. I was so full of shame and fear that I could taste the fear in my throat rushing down to my stomach. There are drug testing kits today that are compact enough to be carried in your pocket. Technology! I prayed for strength to escape this life and be able To secure a sane life for me and my two still very young children.

The main man of this drug ring was a boss in Bed-Stuy. He was a mafia underling. The boss who dressed in his costume of denim overalls also used me to go with him and retrieve bags of heroin that had been dropped off and stashed for pick-up in a metal subway locker I don't think these lockers exist anymore for fear terrorist might plant a bomb. Such is the climate after Bin Laden and 9/11. The drugs were usually placed inside an innocent looking shoe box. Once I returned to the car, I was ordered to place the bags in my underwear. A gun at your head will make you do just about anything. Especially when your family is threatened with death. The boss thought nothing of beating, stomping and making Marty crawl on his knees for drugs. He delighted in doing this in front of me. Trapped once again in hell!

My parents died 5 months apart when I was 22 years old. My daughter was also born that year, 1964. This was also the same year I realized quite by accident that Marty had succumbed and was using heroin. Not a very good year. The little family I had left wouldn't or couldn't help me to get out of the situation.

Before it was all over, this chapter of my journey included constantly moving, living or trying to live on little money. Every breath I took was full of disgrace. I was in love with a broke down, beat up heroin junkie. It's so hard to watch someone you've grown up with, someone who was kind and caring, someone who worked hard and laughed harder, someone so handsome and ambitious falling apart right before your eyes. Finally every thing we worked for and everything thing we owned was lost. I was homeless with two small children.

I was working but I still didn't have enough money for housing. N.Y. is expensive to thrive in. I was able to find shelter for the children. This women asked for so much of my salary, I didn't have much left to save up three months rent for an apartment I asked if I could sleep on her floor, but she said no. I slept on the subway trains and on a bench in the locker room at work. I washed in restrooms. At one point, I was wrongly diagnosed with stomach cancer. I was very sick and run down. For 2 weeks I existed off of water and whatever scraps the kids left. Of course that wasn't much, they were hungry. I reluctantly dragged me and the kids to the welfare office. I was so ashamed because as far as I knew there had never been any other person in my family on welfare.

Going to the welfare office to ask for help turned out to be a life-saver after all. We did live in a few disgusting drug and roach infested, dangerous welfare hotels before we were able to afford an apt. You could be getting on the elevator and witness an addict giving oral sex to a man in a wheel chair, so that he would be able to score his next fix. One night I watched a huge rat quickly scurry across my son's bed. He was asleep and spared the sight and the fright. Roaches were a constant. You may hear the cry of a woman who was getting her ass beat by her pimp because she didn't bring him enough money. There was a short time when Marty pimped about 5 girls who were instructed to bring the money to me. A habit can make you do some strange things. He wasn't cut out for brutalizing women so that didn't last too long. Night after night we would hear a baby wailing the saddest sound I ever heard. Her parents were both strung out. It was so hard to hold on to my sanity. I was able to hold tight to a little hope because I felt if I just kept trying we could rise from this horror.

The guardian angel from the welfare office actually fed us even before we had the papers and forms completed. She really cared and saw our desperation. She also put us on a special program that would continue to help us financially when I started a full time job. This way you had enough money to get an apt. and start your life once again. She even saw to it that the male case worker I had, was replaced by a decent case worker who didn't insist I give him sexual favors when my babies needed shoes. Dirty Blue Eyed Balding Devil. Good riddance!

Marty was always able to find us. He would show up with a big bag of groceries . I didn't make enough money to move far from the neighborhood. The kids were always happy to see him and so was I. With the life he lived, I was forever trying to prepare myself for the news that he had overdosed, or was killed by another drug addict. There were many sleepless nights full of worry. He promised to get on the list for a new drug called methadone that was successful in keeping heroin addicts off heroin. Of course they substituted one drug for another. The government supplied methadone so the other citizens were safer from being hurt and robbed for drug money.

Marty tried over and over again to kick. With the hope of receiving the methadone treatment, we felt this would be the answer. Going "cold turkey", is a horrible sight to see. The excruciating body aches and pains, the vomit, the diarrhea, the screams, the tears. At times I had to literally sit on top of him to hold him down. That didn't always work. The chills and fever consumed him. The methadone list was so long, I couldn't continue to wait it out. The last straw was when I came home from work early, not feeling so well. I walked into my kitchen which was occupied by four addicts with needles sticking in their arms. They sat around my kitchen table in various degrees of ecstasy. Among this group which of course included Marty, was a beautiful young woman who had to be at least 8 months pregnant. What a sad and pitiful image to see. I almost fell to my knees. The same day I found out that Marty had used the kids to go and "cop" his fix from a neighbor, when he was so sick he couldn't go himself. What was I thinking! Loving a mainline heroin addict rocked my health and my self-esteem. Marty was such a sweet soul, still able to be affectionate but still an addict. By now he was mixing heroin with cocaine.

I had to get out of there. I was quickly losing it. I wanted to kill us because I couldn't find a way to make this unbearable pain go away. Since I felt we were dead already, murder/suicide was an easy choice to make. On the day I made the attempt, I closed all openings with towels and clothing. I told the kids to take a nap and I turned the gas on. Hopelessness is a bitch. My son Jai wouldn't go to sleep because he was hungry. I couldn't have him going to "glory" hungry. I decided to get up and fix him a peanut butter and grape jelly sandwich, which he liked a lot. By this time I came to my senses feeling stupid and sorrowful and realized I had to stay alive even if I was dying on the inside. The kids deserved better. Maybe if I kept going a little longer, putting one emotion in front of the other, we would eventually make it out of this nightmare. Jai who loved to eat, saved us from my attempt to make things better in the wrong way. That was my first suicide effort.

The second was after I had already been sexually assaulted 6 times, by strangers, I was raped by a 6ft., 8in. creep I thought I could trust. I couldn't fight him off. Too big, too strong. Sleeping pills. Overdose. My now sister-in-law came over in the nick of time and kept me from going under with repeated showers and a lot of walking, and chucking up. She's been a good friend to me.

I called my brother who now lived in Richmond, Va. He graduated from A&T college in N.C. and settled in Va. with his family. I was in a panic, crying hysterically and lost, in need of help, bad. He and his wife came to Brooklyn and rescued me and the children. Jai was eight and Cheri was seven. I was thirty one but felt one hundred and two.

We started all over again from scratch. We left N.Y. with one suitcase packed with clothes for the three of us. Billy accidentally picked up another suitcase with old family photos instead of the one with more clothes. We were to go back to N.Y. and get the rest of our things and put them in storage in Va., until I had an apt. Meanwhile we stayed at Billy's apt. We didn't go back the following week. Of course by the time we did get back to Brooklyn, all our things were gone. Sold for drugs I'm sure. My furniture at this time was in pretty good condition. I had recently replaced it because our apt. was emptied of all furniture except the children's furniture. I don't know why, maybe there wasn't enough room for it. The refrigerator was also taken. I was robbed while I was at work. I always thought my neighbors may have been involved . They knew I was a single parent. They knew my schedule, and the people that occupied the space of the stoop were job-less, unemployed, sipping and tasting their day away in drunken bliss They said they thought I was moving. They watched everything. The moving van drove up and left before I came home. What a feeling of violation, raped. So we literally started from scratch. I treasure the old photos we came with, pictures of my deceased parents, and my youth. They are the only things I've been able to salvage from my pass.

If some one put their old furniture out on the curb after replacing it with the new, the kids and I would wait until dark and go and gather what we could to help furnish our new Va. apt. Eventually things got better and we were never homeless again.

With my divorce and with my 2nd husband, James Norman, we managed to build a 5 bedroom redwood home in a safer community that was just developing. James came with his demons that he was able to overcome. He was a Vietnam veteran with a problem with alcohol and cocaine. He made the effort to change and succeeded . Thank God! By this time, I was much too weak to fight. James drove an eighteen wheeler up and down the east coast and across the states. Once he settled, he made an effort to be a good provider and partner. We have been together for 33 years now. 30 married.

Of course there were many other experiences that would fall under the heading of trepidation, such as my new next door neighbor being shot dead at his front door. Both Jai and Cheri left me to live with their father in N.Y. Ain't that a bitch! It felt like everything I went through was in vain. They both saw the grass was not greener on the other side, and came back to Va.

I would be writing for 40 years to share it all. As of now, Cherelle Denise is 43 years old, self sufficient master hair stylist, taking care of her beautiful daughter, Cynthia Diana. Martin Wayne Jr. became a paratrooper, 82nd airborne, real estate salesmen and a car salesman who received many honors including an award for "Salesman of the Year". He also became a prolific baby maker. When Jai was shot 5 times and murdered in 1995, he left behind 4 beautiful children. At this time, 3 of them are in my life. Takeshia and Lateshia my twins are 26 years old. Keshia gave birth to Jai's granddaughter, Khamani Makhi, almost 3 yrs ago. What a bundle of delight. I'm a great grandma. Now ain't that something. Lateshia graduated from VCU and is working on her masters in sociology. I find that very interesting because had I not been so traumatized after being abducted by a sexual deviant, who found orgasmic pleasure in ejaculating all over my naked body, I wouldn't have dropped out of Brooklyn College and I would have continued my education studying sociology also. I lived it instead. Keshia has a wonderful husband Matt. He's one of the good guys. Keshia is continually moving upward in her job at the local bank

I had my baby girl with my second husband. Her name is Jaime Nicole. Jaime whose nickname is Aisha is 30 yrs. old, was named after Stevie Wonder's daughter. He sang to his baby girl in a song called "Isn't She Lovely". James insisted we nickname her after Stevie's daughter. And so it was done. Aisha has been a TV talent on "The For Kids Sake ", Saturday morning show in Richmond. She also attended Va. Tech, taught and counseled children academically and spiritually. She continues to attend weekly spiritually orientated gatherings with her "kids". To hear her speak to the congregation at her church filled us with such joy and pride, I'm sure I floated on air for a while. Let me not forget to mention that her natural passion is for photography. Girlfriend is mighty good, if I must say so myself. She has posted a sample of her interesting and creative photos on the internet. I am so thankful for my girls. They are all doing well. I lost communication with Jai's oldest daughter who may also have my second great grandchild. That's my next mission, to find Margaret Diana Scott. I look at her picture everyday and wish her love. Jai's only son Trey, lives in S.C. and just graduated from High School. His plan is to attend A&T college in N.C., my brothers' alma mater. This is also the college the Rev. Jessie Jackson attended. "Trey", Martin Wayne Scott 3rd, is a handsome and charming and tall young man. All his male ancestors were kissed by the Gods, I do believe. I adore him. When I see him, I see in him his Dad, Martin Wayne Scott 2nd, his Grandfather, Martin Wayne Scott 1st., and my handsome Dad, William Ebbert Simkins. Marty my first husband, died with aids, still loving and being loved.

I have search for peace of mind for a long time. I'm moving closer and closer to it. The negative drama has greatly diminished. My life is good. I recently heard someone say they were "Too blessed to be stressed". I like that!

Gone,
Luckie

Made in the USA
Columbia, SC
22 October 2022